This book belongs to Dora Rosa

Y0-BPU-103

Alphabet & Counting

By: Kim Thompson, Ken Carder, & Nancy Wright

Illustrations: Tracy Rapin

Cover Illustration: Tammy Ortner

Easily use these learning songs, worksheets, and activities with kids of all learning styles!

Many kids are **visual learners.** They think in pictures, quickly converting everything they read, see, and hear into images in their mind. Most visual learners can sit still at their desk easily, focus for longer periods of time, and turn in neat, organized work. Visual learners are more comfortable learning from workbooks and textbooks.

Other children are **auditory learners.** These kids don't do what visual learners seem to do naturally. Auditory learners learn best by listening —being read to, listening to audio books, discussing a topic one-on-one with a teacher or within a small group, singing and learning with music and rhythm.

Still other children are **kinesthetic learners** who learn best through a hands-on approach, body movement, activities, arts and crafts, and manipulating objects.

These songs, worksheets and activities are easily adaptable for use both at home or in the classroom. Parents and caregivers may jumpstart or reinforce school learning at home with the fun, family activities. Classroom teachers may adapt the activities and worksheets as a supplement to their curriculum.

www.twinsisters.com

1-800-248-TWIN (8946)

Twin Sisters Productions, LLC • Akron, OH

© 2005 Twin Sisters IP, LLC. All Rights Reserved.

COPYRIGHT
© 2005 Twin Sisters IP, LLC. All Rights Reserved.
Printed in Hong Kong.

The purchase of this material entitles the buyer to reproduce activities, patterns, and worksheets for home or classroom use only—not for commercial resale. Reproduction of these materials for an entire school or school district is prohibited.

Credits:
Publisher: Twin Sisters Productions, LLC
Executive Producers: Kim Mitzo Thompson, Karen Mitzo Hilderbrand
Original Music by: Kim Mitzo Thompson, Hal Wright
Music Arranged by: Hal Wright
The Animal Alphabet Song by: Nancy Wright
Workbook Authors: Kim Thompson, Ken Carder
Illustrations: Tracy Rapin
Cover Illustration: Tammy Ortner
The Animal Alphabet art activity created by:
McKenna Carder (age 7)
and her mother, Tammy Carder
ISBN 1575838192

Twin Sisters Productions, LLC
www.twinsisters.com

About the Authors

Kim Thompson (President, Author)

Kim is first and foremost the proud wife to Scott and mother to three great kids, Austin, Morgan, and Bailey. She and her twin sister, Karen, founded Twin Sisters Productions over 18 years ago. Kim discovered as a classroom teacher that students who had difficulty learning basic skills soon experienced great success learning those concepts with music. Kim remains the driving force behind the development of every educational music resource the company publishes. She is a graduate of The University of Akron with a M.S. in Education, "Integrating the Arts into the Elementary Curriculum."

Ken Carder (Author, Editor)

Ken is a graduate of The University of Akron in Akron, OH with a B.A. in Communication And Rhetoric, and of Evangelical School of Theology in Myerstown, PA with a M.Div. For the past three years Ken has worked exclusively with Twin Sisters Productions to develop new educational music resources for children. He and his wife have worked extensively with young children in churches, summer camps, schools, a syndicated radio ministry broadcast, and community theater. Ken and his wife are proud parents of three children, Stephen, Nathan, and McKenna.

Nancy Roebuck Wright (Teacher, and author of *The Animal Alphabet*)

Nancy is a graduate of Meredith College in Raleigh, NC and a former elementary classroom teacher. The mother of four grown children and grandmom of two grandsons is in her 15th year of teaching four year olds in a Cary, NC preschool. She also teaches art in grades K–2. Nancy's love of nature and her appreciation of art and music are obvious in her classroom. Her students are filled with excitement and discovery as their child-made Animal Alphabet came to life artistically and musically.

Table Of Contents

© 2005 Twin Sisters IP, LLC. All Rights Reserved.

Introduction

Learning to recognize, pronounce, and write the letters of the alphabet is a huge challenge for your preschool and kindergarten age child. Developing and mastering these skills will lay a solid foundation for reading and future academic success. Make learning fun for everyone with the songs, art activities, worksheets, and finger puppets in the **ALPHABET AND COUNTING** Workbook and CD.

Depending upon their age and abilities most four-, five-, and six-year-olds are developing **pre-reading skills.** They are beginning to:

- **Understand that letters are symbols that represent sounds and several letters together may make a word**
- **Match letters to sounds**
- **Identify the initial consonant of a word**
- **Make pictures or words that begin with the same sound**
- **Combine letters to represent words**
- **Show that words may be combined to create sentences**
- **Demonstrate some conventions of print, including top to bottom, left to right, and letter formation.**

Teach the letters of the alphabet in 26 weeks to jumpstart or reinforce preschool and kindergarten learning. Work with one letter each week. Help your child to recognize the uppercase and lowercase letter; how to correctly print the letter; pronounce the sound or sounds the letter usually makes; and say other words that begin with the same letter sound. The songs, *The Animal Alphabet* art activities and finger puppets, learning activities, and worksheets are great tools for learning together each day.

© 2005 Twin Sisters IP, LLC. All Rights Reserved.

Each day, as part of a routine, sing one or more of the Alphabet learning songs on the accompanying music CD. Stand up, move your body, make motions with your hands, smile and laugh together while you sing.

On the first day, work on recognizing and correctly pronouncing the letter. On day two, work together to create *The Animal Alphabet* poster. On the third day, practice writing the letter using the worksheets or a writing tablet. On day four, plan an activity that focuses on the selected letter. Finally, begin to make the connection between the written letters and words and what they represent. Show or discuss words that begin with the letter. At the end of the week, have your child showcase his or her learning accomplishments for the rest of the family!

Many four-, five-, and six-year-olds are **developing early math skills.** Again, depending upon age and abilities, a preschooler or kindergartner may be able to count orally from 1 to 20, and possibly to 100 by ones, fives, and tens. They may be able to match numerals to a set of objects, up to 20, if not higher. Included are fun, easy number and counting activities for you and your child to do together. The Number Poems will provide practice in identifying and writing each number.

Make learning together fun and enjoyable for your preschooler or kindergartner.

Sincerely,

Kim Thompson

Kim Mitzo Thompson

Karen Hilderbrand

Karen Mitzo Hilderbrand

© 2005 Twin Sisters IP, LLC. All Rights Reserved.

Animal Alphabet Art Activity

A-a ALLIGATOR

Did You Know?

Alligators have broad, flat, and rounded snouts and their lower teeth cannot be seen when their mouths are closed.

Make an **Alligator A** from green construction paper. Glue brown triangles for scales and white triangles for teeth. Add details to the feet, tail, arms, and mouth with a black marker.

© 2005 Twin Sisters IP, LLC. All Rights Reserved.

TONGUE twister

Andy Alligator is always all alone.

Trace and write the letter A.

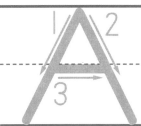

Trace and write the letter a.

The Ants Came Marching...

Create your own army of ants. Press your finger into an inkpad and onto a paper. Place two fingerprints beside each other, touching. Use a marker to add legs and antennae. Write, "A is for Ant."

A is for

© 2005 Twin Sisters IP, LLC. All Rights Reserved.

Animal Alphabet Art Activity

B-b BUMBLEBEE

Use yellow construction paper for the **Bumblebee B.** Add orange construction paper wings and a triangular stinger. Use black marker to add details—mouth, eyes, antennae, and stripes.

Did You Know?

Bumblebees are large, fuzzy, black and yellow-orange bees with dark wings. Bumblebee queens are most often seen visiting flowers in early spring. After her workers hatch, the workers do all of the nectar and pollen gathering while the queen stays in the nest.

© 2005 Twin Sisters IP, LLC. All Rights Reserved.

Betsy Bumblebee is busy
buzzing by the beehive.

Trace and write the letter B.

B

Trace and write the letter b.

b

Alphabet Meal

Work together to make up a menu in which the names of all the foods begin with the letter b.
For example, black beans, burritos, bagels, broccoli, and bubble gum ice cream.

Menu

Black Beans

Broccoli

Burritos

Bagels

Bubble Gum
Ice Cream

9

© 2005 Twin Sisters IP, LLC. All Rights Reserved.

Animal Alphabet Art Activity

C-c CATERPILLAR

Did You Know?

Some caterpillars have eyespots—a circular, eye-like marking found on the body—that make the caterpillar's face look like a bigger, more dangerous snake to scare away some predators.

Cut out an uppercase block letter C. Glue full or half-circles of a contrasting color around the back of the letter C. Glue a small triangle at the end of the C to make a head. Use black marker to add details—eyes, antennae, and texture.

© 2005 Twin Sisters IP, LLC. All Rights Reserved.

Trace and write the letter C.

C

Trace and write the letter c.

c

Hard C and Soft C

Look through catalogs, magazines, and advertisements and cut out pictures of objects that begin with the letter c. Help your child divide the items into two groups: those with a hard c sound, as in cookies, and those with a soft c sound, as in celery.

© 2005 Twin Sisters IP, LLC. All Rights Reserved.

Animal Alphabet
Art Activity

D-d DUCK

Did You Know?
Ducks are common water birds. The adult female duck is called a **hen**, the adult male is called a **drake**, and the young are called **ducklings**.

Cut out an uppercase block letter D. From construction paper of a contrasting color, cut out a wing, tail feather, two feet, an eye, and a bill. Use black marker to add details to each.

© 2005 Twin Sisters IP, LLC. All Rights Reserved.

Diana Duck dances in
her dreams.

Trace and write the letter D.

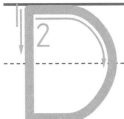

Trace and write the letter d.

Alphabet Tic-Tac-Toe

Instead of using an X and an O, play with lowercase letters b and d, which are among the more difficult letters for children to recognize because they look so similar. Or choose any two letters your child might be having trouble identifying.

13

© 2005 Twin Sisters IP, LLC. All Rights Reserved.

Animal Alphabet Art Activity

E-e ELEPHANT

Did You Know?

An elephant's trunk is actually part nose and part upper lip. Elephants breathe and smell through their trunks. They use the trunk to put food into their mouths, and can even spray water with it!

Use gray construction paper for an uppercase block letter E. Cut out one trunk and two irregular shaped ovals for elephant ears. Use black marker to add details—eyes, outline of the ears, legs, and trunk.

© 2005 Twin Sisters IP, LLC. All Rights Reserved.

TONGUE twister

Elliot Elephant easily eats eighty eggs.

Trace and write the letter E.

Trace and write the letter e.

Short e and Long e

Look through catalogs, magazines, and advertisements together. Cut out pictures of objects whose name begins with or contains the vowel e. Help your child divide the items into two groups: those that contain a short e sound, as in *eggs* and *beds*, and those with a long e sound, as in *eagle* and *cheese*.

© 2005 Twin Sisters IP, LLC. All Rights Reserved.

Animal Alphabet Art Activity

F-f FISH

Did You Know?

Many marine biologists and researchers believe there may be 28,000 different fish species.

Cut out an uppercase block letter F. From construction paper of a contrasting color, cut out a set of "fish lips" and three fins: one the width of the top horizontal, a second the length of the smaller horizontal, and a third the width of the vertical. Add details with a black marker—mouth, eye, gills, and textures. Add stripes to the fish with construction paper, markers, or paint.

© 2005 Twin Sisters IP, LLC. All Rights Reserved.

*Franklin Fish found
fifty fans.*

Trace and write the letter F.

Trace and write the letter f.

Funky Finger Painting

Draw the letter F in large block or outline form on poster board or construction paper.
Fill in the outline by finger painting. Write the letter F, paint fish, footballs, frogs, fireworks,
flowers, fruit, fire, and other objects that begin with the letter F.

© 2005 Twin Sisters IP, LLC. All Rights Reserved.

Animal Alphabet Art Activity

G-g GRASSHOPPER

Did You Know?
When some grasshoppers are picked up, they "spit" a brown liquid which is often called "tobacco juice." Some scientists believe that this liquid may protect grasshoppers from attacks by insects such as ants.

Cut out an uppercase block letter G from green construction paper. Cut out an oval-shaped head, and legs from yellow construction paper. Add details with a black marker—eyes, mouth, antennae, feet, and body markings.

© 2005 Twin Sisters IP, LLC. All Rights Reserved.

Gretel Grasshopper grazes
in the grass.

Trace and write the letter G.

Trace and write the letter g.

Two Of A Kind

Write a row of letters on a sheet of paper. For example,
C, E, G, and D, or M, N, W, and V. Help your child
describe the characteristics of each letter. How are the
letters similar? How are the letters different?

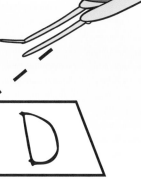

© 2005 Twin Sisters IP, LLC. All Rights Reserved.

Animal Alphabet Art Activity

H-h HORSE

Did You Know?

An adult female horse is called a **mare**; the adult male is called a **stallion**. A **foal** is a horse not yet one year old; a **colt** is a young male and a **filly** is a young female. A **pony** is a small horse, less than 58 inches tall at the shoulder.

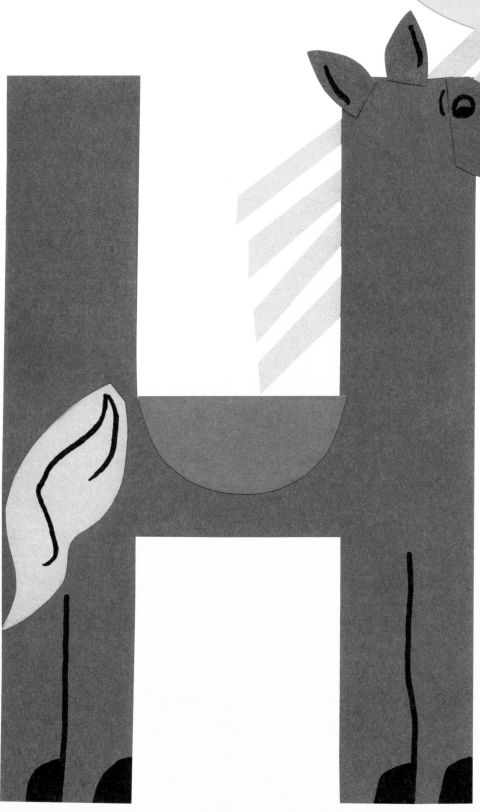

Cut out an uppercase block letter H from brown construction paper. Cut out one small brown oval for the horse's head and two small triangles for the ears. From contrasting construction paper cut out a tail, mane, and saddle. Add details with a black marker—eyes, mouth, nose, ears, legs and hooves, and texture.

© 2005 Twin Sisters IP, LLC. All Rights Reserved.

Henry Horse happily
hides in the haystack.

Trace and write the letter H.

H

Trace and write the letter h.

h

The Hairy Horse Is a Happy Horse

Take turns describing the hairy horse with words that begin with the letter H. "The hairy horse is a happy horse." The next player, in rhythm, might say, "The hairy horse is a hungry horse." Adjectives that begin with H include:

- hopeful
- hopeless
- handsome
- horrible
- homely
- helpful
- helpless

happy
hairy
hopeful

hopeless
handsome

horrible
homely
helpful

21

© 2005 Twin Sisters IP, LLC. All Rights Reserved.

Animal Alphabet Art Activity

I-i INSECT

Did You Know?

All insects have a hard exoskeleton, a three-part body, and three pairs of jointed legs, large compound eyes, and two antennae. There are about a million different types of insects.

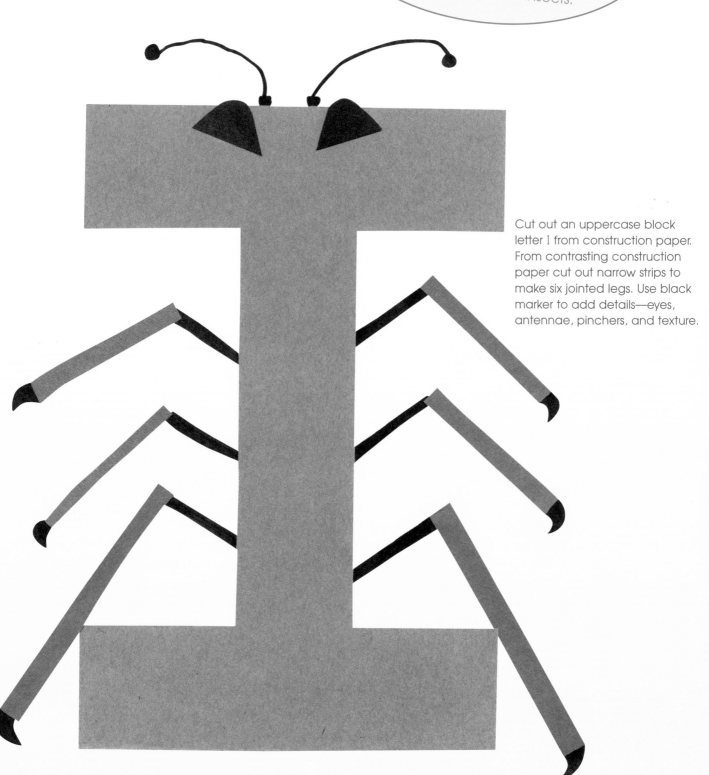

Cut out an uppercase block letter I from construction paper. From contrasting construction paper cut out narrow strips to make six jointed legs. Use black marker to add details—eyes, antennae, pinchers, and texture.

© 2005 Twin Sisters IP, LLC. All Rights Reserved.

Ivana Insect is
in Ireland.

Trace and write the letter I.

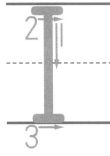

Trace and write the letter i.

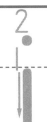

Short i and Long i

Look through catalogs, magazines, and advertisements together. Cut out pictures of objects whose name begins with or contains the vowel i. Help your child divide the items into two groups: those that contain a short i sound, as in *crib, milk,* and *mitten,* and those with a long i sound, as in *ice cream* and *dime.*

For even more learning fun, work together to list as many words as possible in one minute (or any other set time limit) that contain or begin with the short i sound. Repeat at another time making a list of words that begin with or contain the long i sound.

Milk

White
Glue

© 2005 Twin Sisters IP, LLC. All Rights Reserved.

Animal Alphabet Art Activity

J-j JAGUAR

Did You Know?

The jaguar will wait by the water's edge and hit the surface of the water with its tail to attract fish. As the fish come near, the jaguar swats at them, spearing the fish with its sharp claws.

Cut out an uppercase block letter J. From contrasting construction paper, cut out small circles and ovals for the eyes and the mouth; a square for the nose; two triangles for ears; and a long tail. Tear construction paper into small pieces for the spots. Add details to the eyes and mouth with a black marker.

© 2005 Twin Sisters IP, LLC. All Rights Reserved.

TONGUE
twister

Joey Jaguar juggles
jelly jars.

Trace and write the letter J.

Trace and write the letter j.

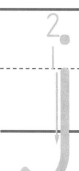

Jean Art

Draw the letter J in large block or outline form on poster
board or cardboard. Fill in the outline by gluing pieces of
old blue jeans cut into small shapes.

© 2005 Twin Sisters IP, LLC. All Rights Reserved.

Animal Alphabet Art Activity

K-k KANGAROO

Did You Know?
There are more than 50 different kinds of kangaroos! Kangaroos can hop up to 40 miles per hour and over 30 feet in one hop.

Cut out an uppercase block letter K and a curly tail from brown construction paper. Cut out a pouch pocket from gray construction paper. From pink construction paper cut out two irregular shaped triangles for ears; and three ovals for paws, each the width of the block letter. Use a black marker to add details—pouch pocket, paws, eyes, ears, and nose.

© 2005 Twin Sisters IP, LLC. All Rights Reserved.

TONGUE twister

Katrina Kangaroo keeps the king's keys.

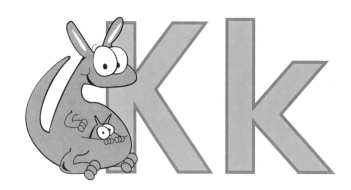

Trace and write the letter K.

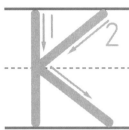

Trace and write the letter k.

Kool-Aid® Art

Draw the letter K in large block or outline form on poster board or cardboard. Spread glue on the letter K. Sprinkle different flavors of powdered Kool-Aid® onto the glue.

© 2005 Twin Sisters IP, LLC. All Rights Reserved.

Animal Alphabet Art Activity

L-l LION

Did You Know?

The female lion does more than 90% of the hunting while the male spends about 20 hours a day resting.

Cut out an uppercase block letter L from brown construction paper. From orange and yellow construction paper cut out a rectangle for the face, two circles for the ears, a triangle for the nose, a curly tail, and several small strips for the mane. Use a black marker to add detail—eyes, mouth, ears, feet, and texture.

© 2005 Twin Sisters IP, LLC. All Rights Reserved.

Leo Lion loves lime
lollipops.

Trace and write the letter L.

Trace and write the letter l.

Digging for Letters

Fill a box or an under-the-bed storage container with sand. Bury a set of magnetic letters in the sand. Ask your child to dig up and identify a letter. For more challenging fun, bury only the uppercase letters in the sand. Help your child to dig up a letter and match it to the lowercase letter on the table.

© 2005 Twin Sisters IP, LLC. All Rights Reserved.

Animal Alphabet Art Activity

M-m MOUSE

Did You Know?

Did you know that a mouse's front teeth continue to grow throughout its life? The mouse must gnaw on hard things to keep wearing the teeth down.

Cut out an uppercase block letter M and a curly tail from gray construction paper. From pink construction paper, cut out a large circle; cut the circle into four quarters and use two quarters for ears. Add details with a black marker—nose, eyes, whiskers, and ears.

© 2005 Twin Sisters IP, LLC. All Rights Reserved.

TONGUE twister
Mandy Mouse munches macaroni and meatballs.

Trace and write the letter M.

M

Trace and write the letter m.

m

Alphabet Roadway

Cut large uppercase and lowercase letters from black construction paper or poster board. Paint yellow road stripes on each letter. Create an alphabet roadway by laying the letters on the floor. Drive toy cars and trucks on the road, identifying each letter along the way.

© 2005 Twin Sisters IP, LLC. All Rights Reserved.

Animal Alphabet
Art Activity

N-n NIGHT CRAWLER

Did You Know?
A night crawler is another name for an earthworm. The earthworm's brain, hearts—it has five—and breathing organs are located in the first few segments of the worm. The rest of the earthworm is filled with the intestines to digest its food.

Cut out an uppercase block letter N from brown construction paper. Cut out an irregular shaped oval for the head and a rounded triangle for the end of the night crawler. Add details with a black marker— eyes, mouth, and wrinkles.

© 2005 Twin Sisters IP, LLC. All Rights Reserved.

TONGUE
twister
Nathan Night crawler never naps at night.

Trace and write the letter N

Trace and write the letter n

Rainbow Letters

Ask your child to write uppercase letters across a line of tablet paper using a pencil. Trace the line of letters with a different colored pencil. Repeat this step with several colored pencils to create rainbow letters.

© 2005 Twin Sisters IP, LLC. All Rights Reserved.

O-o OWL

Did You Know?

Owls cannot move their eyes within their sockets. In order to look around, they have to move their entire head.

Cut out an uppercase block letter O from brown construction paper. From contrasting construction paper cut out the following: two pointed ovals for wings; a triangle for the beak; an irregular shaped rectangle for the tail feathers; two circles and two starbursts for eyes; and small triangles for wing feathers. Use black marker to outline the feathers and add details—eyes and beak.

© 2005 Twin Sisters IP, LLC. All Rights Reserved.

TONGUE
twister

Ollie Owl often offers
others Olives.

Trace and write the letter O.

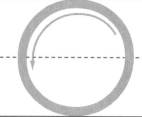

Trace and write the letter o.

Short o and Long o Search

Look through catalogs, magazines, and advertisements together. Cut out pictures of objects whose name begins with or contains the vowel o. Help your child divide the items into two groups: those that contain a short o sound, as in *box* and *otter*, and those with a long o sound, as in *boat* and *robe*.

For even more learning fun, read a favorite book together! Afterwards, help your child to find words in the book that contain the letter o. Divide a piece of paper into two columns labeled "short o" and "long o." Help your child write the words in the correct columns. Play this game with other vowels, too.

© 2005 Twin Sisters IP, LLC. All Rights Reserved.

Animal Alphabet Art Activity

P-p PIG

Did You Know?

Pigs are also called **hogs** or **swine**. The adult female is called a **sow**. The adult male is called a **boar**. A baby is called a **piglet**. Pigs vary in color from brown, black, white, to pink.

From pink construction paper cut out an uppercase block letter P, two curly ears, one very curly tail, and an oval snout. With a black marker outline the tail and ears, and add other details—eyes, snout, and hooves.

© 2005 Twin Sisters IP, LLC. All Rights Reserved.

Penelope Pig prefers pepperoni pizza and prunes.

Trace and write the letter P.

Trace and write the letter p.

Letter of the Day

Select a letter to look for throughout the day. Write the selected letter on construction paper or copy paper and post it on the refrigerator. Ask your child to search for that letter. Each time she finds the letter—on boxes, magazines, coloring pages, television commercials and other places—she must return and write the letter on the paper displayed on the refrigerator.

© 2005 Twin Sisters IP, LLC. All Rights Reserved.

Animal Alphabet Art Activity

Q-q QUAIL

Did You Know?

The California quail is a common bird from the western United States. They live in woodlands, desert edges, and grassy valleys. Quails live in groups of 10 to 20 birds, called coveys.

Cut out an uppercase block letter Q. From contrasting construction paper cut out the head, beak, wing, leg, large tail feathers, and triangles and circles for smaller feathers—refer to the illustration. Add details with a black marker—eyes, claws, and feathers.

© 2005 Twin Sisters IP, LLC. All Rights Reserved.

Queen Quail quickly quit quarreling.

Trace and write the letter Q.

Trace and write the letter q.

Alphabet Quilt

Cut 28 squares from fabric scraps or remnants. Use black marker or fabric paint to outline one letter of the alphabet on each square. Fill in the outlined letter with fabric or craft paint. Sew all the squares together, 4 squares across and 7 squares down. Note: you'll have two blank squares—add your child's name and the date or some other design.

A	B	C	D
E	F	G	H
I	J	K	L
M	N	O	P
Q	R	S	T
U	V	W	X
Name Here	Y	Z	Date Here

© 2005 Twin Sisters IP, LLC. All Rights Reserved.

Animal Alphabet
Art Activity

R-r RABBIT

Did You Know?
Rabbits and hares are not really one and the same. Rabbits are born naked and blind; hares are born with fur and the ability to see. Rabbits live in underground burrows with many other rabbits. Hares build simple nests and generally live alone!

Cut out an uppercase block letter R. From pink or contrasting construction paper cut out two rabbit ears, one puffy tail, and a circle nose. Add details with a black marker—eyes, mouth, whiskers, ears, and texture.

© 2005 Twin Sisters IP, LLC. All Rights Reserved.

Robbie Rabbit runs rapidly from the rats.

Trace and write the letter R.

Trace and write the letter r.

Me Words

Write your child's first name on a large piece of paper. Ask him to think of one or more words beginning with each letter in his first name. Each word should describe him. For example, Michael may choose the words: musical, intelligent, cute, honest, artist, explorer and loving. Repeat using the names of other family members.

Musical
Intelligent
Cute
Honest
Artistic
Explorer
Loving

musical intelligent cute honest artistic explorer loving

© 2005 Twin Sisters IP, LLC. All Rights Reserved.

Animal Alphabet Art Activity

S-s SALAMANDER

Did You Know?

Salamanders have no scales, claws or external ear openings. Most have four short legs with four toes on each of the front legs, and five toes on each of the hind legs. As salamanders grow they lose the outer layer of their old skin and eat it.

Cut out an uppercase block letter S. From contrasting construction paper cut out four legs, a head and "mane," a curly "tail," and small squares for texture. Add details with a black marker. Refer to the illustration.

© 2005 Twin Sisters IP, LLC. All Rights Reserved.

Sam Salamander Slides
Safely in School.

Trace and write the letter S.

Trace and write the letter s.

String Art

Draw the letter S in large block or outline form on poster board or construction paper. Cut different colors of thick string or yarn into a variety of lengths. Glue the string pieces to the outlined letter S. Make interesting patterns or try to fill the outline using only string S's.

© 2005 Twin Sisters IP, LLC. All Rights Reserved.

Animal Alphabet Art Activity

T-t TURTLE

Did You Know?

Sea turtles cannot pull their head and legs into the shell. They can grow up to 6-feet long and weigh up to 1900 pounds. Adult female sea turtles return to the beach where they were born to lay eggs in the sand.

From green construction paper cut out an uppercase block letter T, two small legs, a triangle tail, and a half-circle head. Make the turtle shell from contrasting construction paper from a half-circle the width of the horizontal. Decorate the shell with different colored circles, triangles, squares, and other shapes. Use black marker to add details—mouth, eyes, claws, and texture.

© 2005 Twin Sisters IP, LLC. All Rights Reserved.

Tony Turtle tells
tall tales.

Trace and write the letter T.

Trace and write the letter t.

3-D Letters

Put moist sand in a box or small plastic storage container. Write wide, deep letters in the sand using your finger. Mix plaster of paris (available at discount and craft stores) according to the package directions and pour into the letter shapes. Let the letters dry. Remove the letters from the sand and paint them with tempera or acrylic paint.

© 2005 Twin Sisters IP, LLC. All Rights Reserved.

Animal Alphabet Art Activity

U-u UNICORN

Did You Know?
The unicorn is a mythical animal that looks like a horse but has a single, twisted horn on the center of its forehead. Unicorns are often used a symbols of purity. Some people think that the unicorn legend was based upon the **oryx**, a long-horned African antelope.

Cut out an uppercase block letter U. From white construction paper, cut out a horse's head and legs. Cut out a mane, horn, and curly tail from contrasting paper. Use a black marker to add details—outline the horn, mane, tail, legs, hooves, mouth, nose, and eyes.

© 2005 Twin Sisters IP, LLC. All Rights Reserved.

Ursula Unicorn Uses
Unusual Umbrellas.

Trace and write the letter U.

Trace and write the letter u.

Short u and Long u Search

Look through catalogs, magazines, and advertisements together. Cut out pictures of objects whose name begins with or contains the vowel u. Help your child divide the items into two groups: those that contain a short u sound, as in *umbrella* and *underwear,* and those with a long u sound, as in *unicorn* and *glue.*

For more fun with the letter u, go on a "u" hunt! As you drive around town, help your child look for the letter "u" in words that appear on building and street signs, billboards, trucks, and cars. Ask your child to identify if the word contains a short or long u sound. Play this game with other vowels, too.

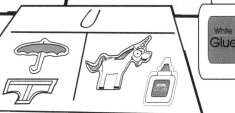

© 2005 Twin Sisters IP, LLC. All Rights Reserved.

Animal Alphabet Art Activity

V-v VULTURE

Did You Know?

Vultures have broad, strong wings and are powerful flyers even though they have the slowest wing beat of any bird—one wing beat per second.

Cut out an uppercase block letter V. From contrasting construction paper cut out the wing feathers, head, beak, head feathers, and claws. Add details to the head, feathers, and claws with a black marker.

© 2005 Twin Sisters IP, LLC. All Rights Reserved.

Vinnie Vulture Views
Videos and Visits Volcanoes.

Trace and write the letter V.

Trace and write the letter v.

Alphabet Pasta

Empty a box of alphabet pasta—available at most grocery stores—into a large bowl. Help your child sort the pasta by letter. Is any letter missing? Are there more of one letter than of another letter? Can you make simple words using the pasta letters?

BOY   FUN   CAT

© 2005 Twin Sisters IP, LLC. All Rights Reserved.

Animal Alphabet Art Activity

W-w WORM

Did You Know?

Earthworms—also called night crawlers—help to create good soil by burrowing deep and leaving behind their waste! Did you know that good soil may have as many as one million worms per acre? Earthworms grow from a few inches long to over 22-feet long.

Cut out an uppercase block letter W and round the edges.
Add details with a black marker—eyes, mouth, and wrinkles.

© 2005 Twin Sisters IP, LLC. All Rights Reserved.

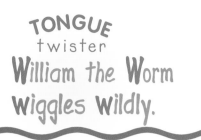

TONGUE
twister
William the Worm
Wiggles Wildly.

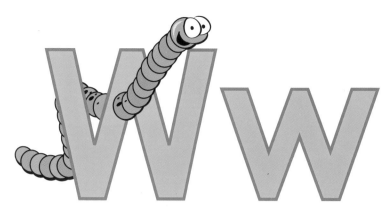

Trace and write the letter W.

Trace and write the letter w.

Substitute Letters

On a sheet of paper, write "b _ g" three times. Write the lowercase a in the blank of the first word to make the word *bag*. Read the word together. Write the lowercase i and u in the other two words. Continue with other word forms such as "c _ t" and "h _t". For more challenging learning fun, ask your child to supply the missing letters.

© 2005 Twin Sisters IP, LLC. All Rights Reserved.

Animal Alphabet
Art Activity

X-x X-RAY FISH

Did You Know?

The x-ray fish is almost transparent so you can actually see inside its body. This South American fish is often kept in freshwater tropical aquariums.

Cut out an uppercase block letter X, two fins, and two lips. From contrasting construction paper, cut out two long, narrow strips and several shorter, narrow strips. Add details with a black marker.

© 2005 Twin Sisters IP, LLC. All Rights Reserved.

TONGUE
twister

Xavier the X-ray fish
eXamines Xylophones.

Trace and write the letter X.

Trace and write the letter x.

Alphabet Dot-to-Dot

Play this simple game on a placemat while waiting at a restaurant. Randomly write the letters of the alphabet. See how quickly your child can connect the letters in the correct order. Begin with only uppercase letters. For more challenging play, add lowercase letters and connect A to a, B to b, and so on.

© 2005 Twin Sisters IP, LLC. All Rights Reserved.

Animal Alphabet Art Activity

Y-y YELLOW JACKET

Did You Know?

Yellow Jackets live and work together in groups called **colonies**. **Queens** are large females who build the nest and lay eggs; **workers** are small females who build nests and feed the young, and males are called **drones**.

From yellow construction paper, cut out an uppercase block letter Y. Use contrasting construction paper to make a circle head, triangle stinger, and half-circle wings. Use a black marker to add stripes, antennae, eyes, and other features.

© 2005 Twin Sisters IP, LLC. All Rights Reserved.

TONGUE
twister

Yasmine the Yellow jacket
Yawns and Yells.

Trace and write the letter Y.

1 Y 2

Trace and write the letter y.

1 y 2

Alphabet March

Place alphabet cards on the floor forming a circle. Play your favorite song while your child steps on each alphabet card. When you stop the music he must freeze in place and say the name of the letter he is standing on. Remove that letter, and repeat until only one special letter remains.

© 2005 Twin Sisters IP, LLC. All Rights Reserved.

Animal Alphabet Art Activity

Z-z ZEBRA

Did You Know?
A zebra is really white with black stripes! No two zebras have stripes that are exactly alike.

Cut out an uppercase block letter Z and a short tail from black construction paper. Cut out several short, narrow strips for the mane. From white construction paper, cut out several small triangles, stripes, and an elongated head with rounded corners. Refer to the illustration.

© 2005 Twin Sisters IP, LLC. All Rights Reserved.

TONGUE
twister

**Zoe Zebra Zips
Zippers at the Zoo.**

Trace and write the letter Z.

Z

Trace and write the letter z.

z

Letters All Around

Try to find letters of the alphabet by looking closely at objects all around us. Spot the Y in a tree branch, the A in the frame of a swing set, or the H in a door molding. See how many letters you can find in or around your house or during a walk around the neighborhood.

© 2005 Twin Sisters IP, LLC. All Rights Reserved.

Uppercase and Lowercase Alphabet Card Games

Carefully cut apart the Uppercase and Lowercase Alphabet Cards on pages 59–63.

Alphabet Hide 'n Seek

Ask your child to search for the alphabet cards you've hidden around the room or the house. As he finds each alphabet card he must bring it to you and identify the letter.

Do You Hear What I Hear?

Say a word aloud. Have your child find and hold up the alphabet card that matches the beginning sound of that word. For more challenging fun, have your child find and hold up the alphabet card that matches the ending sound of that word or the vowel sound in that word.

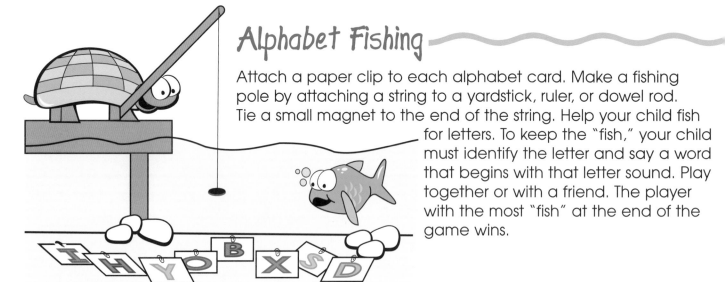

Alphabet Fishing

Attach a paper clip to each alphabet card. Make a fishing pole by attaching a string to a yardstick, ruler, or dowel rod. Tie a small magnet to the end of the string. Help your child fish for letters. To keep the "fish," your child must identify the letter and say a word that begins with that letter sound. Play together or with a friend. The player with the most "fish" at the end of the game wins.

Alphabet Actions

Select several alphabet cards and challenge your child to think of verbs or action words that begin with those letters. With actions in mind, have her act out the word as you try to guess the action.

Alphabet Shopping

Select several alphabet cards and challenge your child to make a shopping list of items to purchase that begin with those letters. Play together or with a friend to see who can make the longest list.

Missing Letter

Place the uppercase or lowercase alphabet cards face up in the correct sequence. Remove several alphabet cards. Ask your child to identify the missing letters.

© 2005 Twin Sisters IP, LLC. All Rights Reserved.

A B C D

E F G H

I J K L

M N O P

Q R S T

Helpful Hint: For sturdier cards, glue entire page on a piece of poster board.
When the glue is dry, cut out the letters.

© 2005 Twin Sisters IP, LLC. All Rights Reserved.

© 2005 Twin Sisters IP, LLC. All Rights Reserved.

This page intentionally left blank.

U V W X

Y Z a b

c d e f

g h i j

k l m n

© 2005 Twin Sisters IP, LLC. All Rights Reserved.

© 2005 Twin Sisters IP, LLC. All Rights Reserved.

This page intentionally left blank.

o	p	q	r
s	t	u	v
w	x	y	z

How to make the Mini-Books

1. Carefully tear out each page.
2. Cut each page on the dotted line.
3. Put the pages in the correct order.
4. Staple along the left edge or punch holes along the edge. Then thread yarn, and tie.

© 2005 Twin Sisters IP, LLC. All Rights Reserved.

© 2005 Twin Sisters IP, LLC. All Rights Reserved.

This page intentionally left blank.

The Animal Alphabet

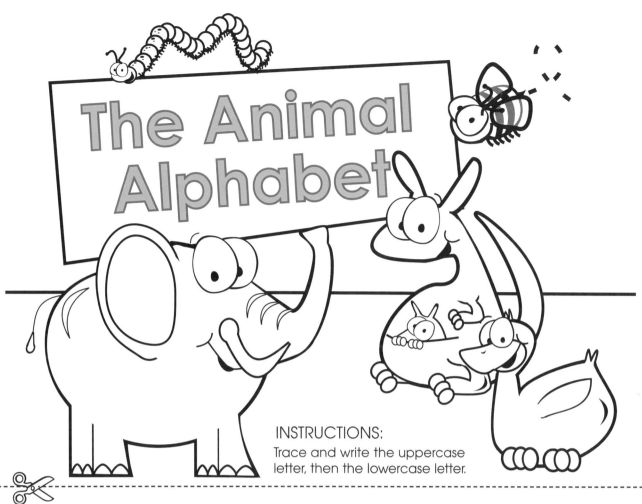

INSTRUCTIONS:
Trace and write the uppercase letter, then the lowercase letter.

Bb

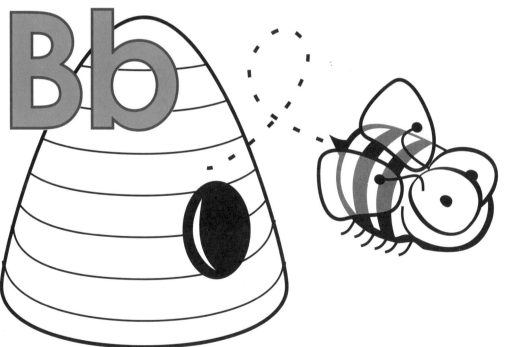

© 2005 Twin Sisters IP, LLC. All Rights Reserved.

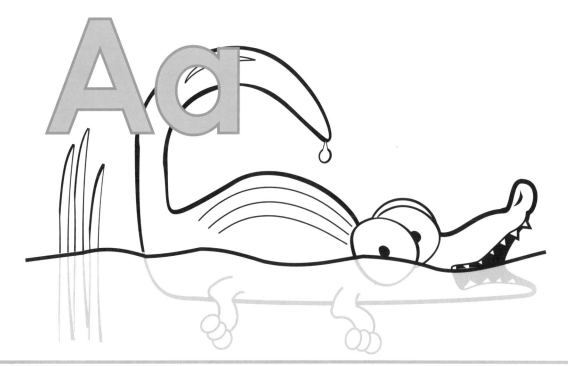

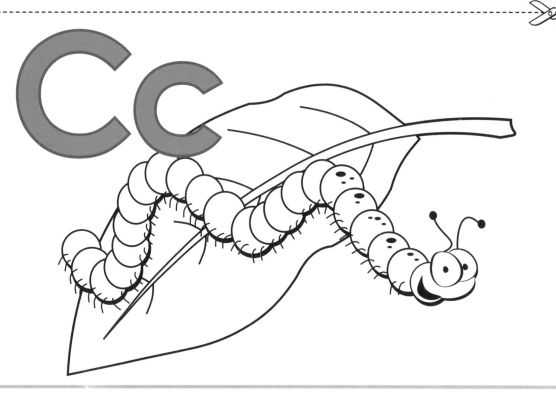

© 2005 Twin Sisters IP, LLC. All Rights Reserved.

Dd

Ff

© 2005 Twin Sisters IP, LLC. All Rights Reserved.

Ee

E
2
3
4

e

G g

G

g

© 2005 Twin Sisters IP, LLC. All Rights Reserved.

© 2005 Twin Sisters IP, LLC. All Rights Reserved.

Ii

Kk

© 2005 Twin Sisters IP, LLC. All Rights Reserved.

Ll

Nn

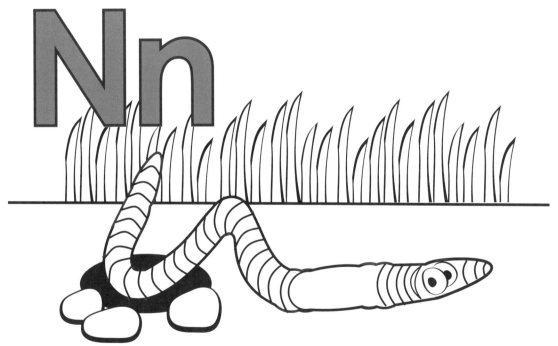

© 2005 Twin Sisters IP, LLC. All Rights Reserved.

© 2005 Twin Sisters IP, LLC. All Rights Reserved.

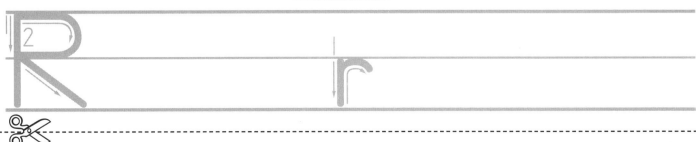

© 2005 Twin Sisters IP, LLC. All Rights Reserved.

Qq

Ss

© 2005 Twin Sisters IP, LLC. All Rights Reserved.

Tt

Vv

© 2005 Twin Sisters IP, LLC. All Rights Reserved.

Uu

U u

Ww

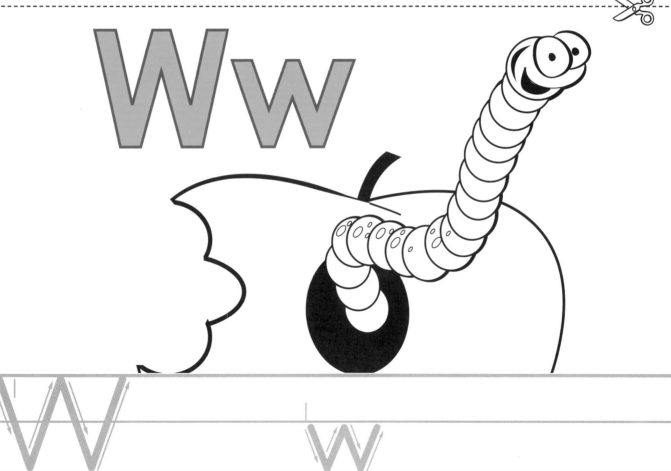

W w

© 2005 Twin Sisters IP, LLC. All Rights Reserved.

© 2005 Twin Sisters IP, LLC. All Rights Reserved.

Aa Bb Cc Dd Ee Ff Gg Hh Ii Jj Kk Ll Mm Nn Oo Pp Qq Rr Ss Tt Uu Vv Ww Xx Yy Zz

The End

© 2005 Twin Sisters IP, LLC. All Rights Reserved.

Number Activities

I Spy a Number!

Walk together through the house, grocery store, or the neighborhood searching for objects that feature numbers—appliances, clocks, calendars, boxes and containers, house numbers, street signs.

Nuts & Bolts

Gather nuts and bolts in assorted sizes. Ask your child to choose one bolt, cover it with nuts, and then count the nuts. Do this with several bolts. Order the bolts from the one with the fewest nuts to the one with the most.

Jellybean Math

Pass out twenty jellybeans. Count the jellybeans aoud together. Have your child sort each color jellybean into a separate pile. Ask your child to count red jellybeans. Then sort green, yellow, pink, and so on. Help your child make patterns using the jellybeans. For example, pink, pink, green, white, pink, pink, green, white. Make up story problems your child can answer by manipulating the jellybeans. For example, "You have five red jellybeans. Take away three red jellybeans. How many red jellybeans do you have now?" Of course, you can both eat a few of the jellybeans, too!

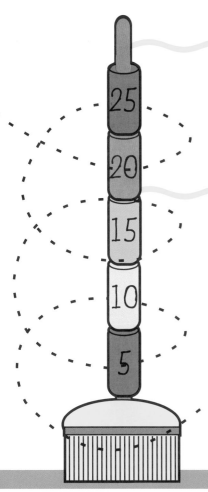

Broomstick Counting

Make simple paper tubes out of construction paper. Label each tube with a number—one to twenty, by fives or tens to one hundred, etc. Challenge your child to slide the tubes onto the handle of a broomstick in numerical order.

Ball Bounce Math

Once your child understands the concept of basic addition, play "Ball Bounce Math." Tell your child to listen carefully as you bounce a ball. Ask your child how many times the ball bounced. Tell your child you're going to bounce the ball a few more times, pause, and then bounce the ball several more times. He will need to tell you how many times the ball bounced. Practice a few simple examples.

© 2005 Twin Sisters IP, LLC. All Rights Reserved.

Number Card Games

Cut out the number cards on page 81. For more fun learning, you'll need to make a color copy of the number cards before cutting the cards apart.

Number Memory Match

Place each card face down on the table. Take turns lifting two cards, trying to find the pair. The player with the most pairs is the winner. **Note:** *You'll need to make color copies of the number cards before cutting them apart.*

Counting Scavenger Hunt

Spread out the number cards face down on a table. Flip over a card and identify the number. Help your child collect that number of small objects from the playroom, kitchen, or family room—wherever you designate. For example, she might collect and count three spoons, five plastic cups, etc.

Number Hide 'n Seek

Ask your child to search for the number cards you've hidden around the room or the house. As he finds each number card he must bring it to you and identify the number.

Missing Number

Place the number cards face up in the correct sequence. Remove several number cards. Ask your child to identify the missing numbers.

Number Fishing

Attach a paper clip to each number card. Make a fishing pole by attaching a string to a yardstick, ruler, or dowel rod. Tie a small magnet to the end of the string. Help your child fish for numbers. Your child must identify the number to keep the "fish." For more challenging play, your child must count aloud up to the number she has caught. Play together or with a friend. The player with the most "fish" at the end of the game wins.

© 2005 Twin Sisters IP, LLC. All Rights Reserved.

1	2	3	4
5	6	7	8
9	10	11	12
13	14	15	16
17	18	19	20

© 2005 Twin Sisters IP, LLC. All Rights Reserved.

© 2005 Twin Sisters IP, LLC. All Rights Reserved.

This page intentionally left blank.

A straight line down and then you're done. It is FUN to make a 1!

Around and around then you'll see how easy it is to make a 3!

© 2005 Twin Sisters IP, LLC. All Rights Reserved.

Go right around then across the ground!

The number 2 is easy, I've found!

2

Down and over, then a simple line —

You've made a 4 and it's mighty fine!

4

© 2005 Twin Sisters IP, LLC. All Rights Reserved.

Down and around,
then a line
on top—
you've made a 5
and now can stop!

From left to right
make a line on top.

Swing down
to the ground—
it's a 7 —so stop!

© 2005 Twin Sisters IP, LLC. All Rights Reserved.

Make a curve, then a loop. That's it. You're done! The number 6 is lots of fun!

Make an S, keep going back up to the top.

You've made an 8 and now can stop!

© 2005 Twin Sisters IP, LLC. All Rights Reserved.

Make a loop and then a line.

That's the way to make a 9.

© 2005 Twin Sisters IP, LLC. All Rights Reserved.

Make a 1, then a 0
right by its side
And the number 10 will appear with pride.

© 2005 Twin Sisters IP, LLC. All Rights Reserved.